Sex, Drugs, and the S.A.T.

Getting out of High School and Getting in to College

Ginger Walsh Cobb and Kathleen Glynn-Sparrow

ISBN: 978-1514158753

Typesetting and cover design by FormattingExperts.com

Acknowledgments

We are grateful for the support of our families over the many years it took for us to write this book. We would also like to thank St. Andrew's Episcopal School and Stone Ridge School of the Sacred Heart for their help in making this book a reality.

Introduction

About the Guide:

Teenagers today text instead of talk and blog instead of blab. So how do you communicate with them about two key life journeys: getting out of high school and getting in to college? *Sex, Drugs and the S.A.T.: Getting out of High School and Getting in to College* will be your road map for these daunting journeys. The authors offer practical solutions for how to address potential roadblocks or crises with your teenager before they happen. And while you're handling the harrowing highways of high school, the authors will steer you and your teenager through the college application process. From how to prevent teenage drinking at parties to crafting a clever college essay, this book will give parents savvy solutions to surviving the teenage years.

Until now, there has not been a book which offers real-life, timely advice to parents about strategies for navigating the tumultuous waters of high school *and* tested guidance on weathering the complex college process. There are books which offer stale statistics about high school social problems and others which counsel on how to write the winning college application essay, but none offer dynamic dialogues with the parents on what to do *right now* with the challenges they are facing with their teenagers during high school. Other authors toss around theories on why teenagers make the choices they do while these authors *understand* why teenagers make those choices because they are working with teenagers every day. The advice given is culled from a combined forty-six years of practical experience guiding teenagers and parents. Yet, this is not outdated advice from authors who have worked previously with teens and their families, but rather from two professionals currently ensconced in the classroom and in administration. This book does not rely on staged interviews or a few counseling sessions with a limited number of students; it is based on real-life experience, "living research."

Sex, Drugs and the S.A.T. will appeal to parents of high school students of all ages. Parents with incoming freshmen will utilize the text as a manual for managing the transition to high school. Parents of rising juniors and seniors will use this book as their go-to-guide for the college process. As helpful as guidance and college counselors are, they cannot be available to answer every detailed question a parent has about high school or the application process. This is where the book can act as a stand-in counselor who is available 24/7...no need to hire a pricey private counselor! And for those questions that seem too trivial or embarrassing to ask a counselor, parents can simply flip to the chapter for stress-easing answers. Remember the number one bestseller *What to Expect When You are Expecting* by Heidi Murkoff and Sharon Mazel? Well, *Sex, Drugs and the S.A.T.* is the teenage version, a *What to Expect During the Teenage Years*.

You might be thinking at this point, "An advice book

sounds boring to read!" And you are right: many parenting books are as invigorating as standing in line at the Motor Vehicle Administration. But *Sex, Drugs and the S.A.T.* will regale you with true but shocking stories about what real teenagers are doing nowadays and offers tested solutions for preventing your teenager from making those same mistakes. It may also keep *you* out of trouble! Did you know that if your teenager throws a party at your house without your knowledge, you could lose your house or be tossed in jail? And the college portion of the book will bring you right up-to-date with major changes in the college process. Did you know that colleges keep track of how many times your teenager contacts the college, and these contacts factor into the admissions decision? Knowing the new gamesmanship involved in the process could turn into college acceptance!

So why do the authors have all the answers? They are well-respected, time-tested professionals who are still active in their fields of expertise. They have the insider's view because they are literally *inside* the schools every day. And, they are working in two prestigious private schools in Montgomery County, Maryland, an affluent area just outside of Washington, D.C. Parents in this area have high expectations, and they want only the best. Ginger Walsh Cobb holds a B.A. in English from Denison University and an M.A. in Private School Leadership from Columbia University. Currently, Ginger is finishing her twenty-second year at St. Andrew's Episcopal School in Potomac, Maryland. As Head of Upper School, she educates students and their families about the following: drug and alcohol abuse, stress, harassment,

Internet safety, eating disorders, relationships and depression. Ginger has helped teenagers for twenty-eight years. Kathleen Glynn-Sparrow holds a B.A. from Duke University and a M.Ed. from Emory University. Kathleen served as Director of College Counseling at St. Andrew's Episcopal School in Potomac, MD. Currently, she is the Associate Director of College Counseling at Stone Ridge School of the Sacred Heart in Bethesda, MD. She also runs The College Coaches, a counseling service which guides families through the college process. Kathleen has advised students from prestigious college preparatory schools all over the Washington, D.C. area. She has spent 18 years in school leadership positions and 15 years counseling families about the college process.

Sex, Drugs, and the S.A.T.: Getting out of High School and Getting in to College is the everything-you-need-to-know-but-won't-ask guide to high school. The road map has changed since you were a teenager: don't you want to know how to travel with your teen on these new roads with the fewest bumps along the way? Be in the driver's seat and take the wheel so you don't let chance steer you wrong. Be informed and be a better driver on these windy roads through high school with *Sex, Drugs, and the S.A.T.* as your GPS.

How to Use This Guide:

Use this book as a reference. Instead of reading it cover to cover, we suggest checking the Table of Contents for the topic you need at the moment. Read that chapter and implement the suggestions offered.

Table of Contents

Part One: Getting out of High School

Top 10 Mistakes Parents Make and How to Fix Them

Oops! I did it again!

As educators, we see many mistakes that parents make over and over because of their inexperience dealing with teenagers. Here are the top 10.

Communication

I never realized it was so hard to talk to a teenager!

Teenagers don't like talking to their parents and rarely want to be seen with them. So how do you crack the teenage code and communicate? Examples and advice are given here.

Drugs/Alcohol

I drank in high school. How bad could it be?

The current research on drugs/alcohol and the brain will show you how times have truly changed.

Chapter 8

Sex

Who wants to discuss sex with a teenager?

While no one likes to discuss sex with teenagers, it is necessary. Tips on how to approach this topic are in this chapter.

Chapter 9 39

Sports/Activities

Aren't academics more important?

A healthy teen should get exercise and be involved in activities to feel more a part of the school and community.

Chapter 10 43

Internet Issues

I can barely handle keeping up with all the Facebook settings, so how am I going to tell what my teen is doing on the computer!

Ideas on how to keep up with the ever-changing internet and who to turn to for help.

Chapter 11 47

Time Management

When does my teen get to breathe?

The over-scheduled teenager can make for a disastrous high school experience and often results in pre-college burnout. There are ways to cut down on the number of activities and still be competitive in college admissions.

Part Two: Getting in to College

Chapter 19
Testing

Does it really matter?

SAT or ACT? When? How Should I Prep? What if my teenager is a poor tester? Read on to boost your test-taking IQ.

Chapter 20
Finding a Good Fit

College talk and cocktails don't mix

It is better to go for a good fit with a college rather than a brand name. Bragging rights are much less important in the long run than a happy teenager.

Chapter 21
Tips for Visiting College Campuses

Looking beyond the cute tour guide

Have coffee in the cafeteria to get a sampling of what the students are like—not just those hand-picked by Admissions to give your tour. Pick up a college newspaper to see the issues students are fired up about, but Admissions isn't mentioning.

Did you know that colleges often look more closely at the short answer responses because they know the applicant did not have help writing them whereas most have coaching on the essay? Read on for more insider tips.

Learn about the new gamesmanship involved in the process and how to strategize!

Now you've done it. Now we'll tell you what to do to fix it!

The brave new world of online applications: its perks and its perils demystified.

Chapter 30 95

Worst Case Scenario

Need we say more?

Your teen was rejected everywhere? Or wants to defer? Follow our advice for a solid Plan B.

Chapter 31 97

Financial Aid and Scholarships

You expect me to PAY for this?

Learn when to apply for aid and discover which colleges may offer more money.

Chapter 32 99

Early Action/Early Decision

Do they have a Late or Really Late Plan?

The mysteries of the many application deadlines are unraveled before your very eyes.

Appendixes

Part One:

Getting out of High School

Chapter 1

Top 10 Mistakes Parents Make and How to Fix Them

"Oops! I did it again!"

1. **Never letting your teen struggle or fail.** Allowing your teen to fail gives him/her a sense of what he or she needs to work on to improve.

2. **Overscheduling your teen.** Teach your teen how to balance his/her life. Exercise, extra-curricular activities, social life, and homework are important but not at the expense of sleep and your teen's health.

3. **Never talking to your teen.** Make time to talk and listen to your teen. Have a special dinner together without cell phones or other electronics!

4. **Not letting your teen assume responsibility when things go wrong.** Learning how to own up to one's mistakes is a vital life skill. Don't make excuses when your teen makes a mistake.

5. **Assuming your teen learned all he or she needed to know about sex in health class.** Teens need to know their parents' values and how to manage relationships.

6. **Assuming your opinion doesn't matter.** While teens are at school or with friends for the majority of their time, their parents' opinions still matter the most. Let your teen know what is important to you and why.

7. **Never carving out time for you and your teen without technology.** Teens crave their parents' attention. Make time for your teen so your teen doesn't try to grab your attention in a negative manner.

8. **Never truly listening to your teen.** Don't assume you have all the answers for your teen. The issues you dealt with as a teen may not be the same issues your teen is struggling to overcome.

9. **Hovering too much.** Give your teen independence. Don't run interference for your child. If your teen is having a problem with a teacher, let your teen have a conversation with the teacher first before you intervene.

10. **Believing your teen would never lie to you.** Many teens lie because they don't want to disappoint you. Stick to your instincts! If what your teen says doesn't add up, investigate.

Chapter 2

Communication

"I never realized it was so hard to talk to a teenager!"

Anecdote

Rodney was a senior in high school before his parents discovered he had a drinking problem. Unfortunately by then, he didn't want to talk to or listen to his parents. His parents had to take extreme measures because there was no communication. Trust was lost on both sides and the only way to regain a trusting relationship was through outside intervention.

Discussion

It is important to have a time set aside to spend with your child. Ideally, you should begin this open communication when your child is in middle school (6th Grade), so when your child begins going to parties, you already have time and space for conversation. Tackle the hard conversations like sex, depression, stress, drinking and drugs early on. Some parents plan private dinners with each of their children so it is a special occasion but also a productive dialogue. Others plan special family time on the weekends such as a walk every Sunday to foster a space for discussion.

Advice

- Preview what topics you want to cover with your child a day or two ahead of time.

- Think or Google examples of the topics you want to cover so you are discussing in the third person.

- Don't expect your child to feel the same way you do about issues. Sometimes it takes several conversations for your child to see things in the same light as you.

Example

If you are going to discuss alcohol, Google articles involving teens and alcohol. Use those examples to get a discussion going. Discuss the dangers of drinking and the ways to avoid them. Ask your teen what he/she will do if he/she is offered alcohol. What if his/her best friend is experimenting? How will your teen tackle these issues? How will they be handled in your home? As a parent, where do you stand on these issues?

Chapter 3

Drugs/Alcohol

"I drank in high school. How bad could it be?"

Anecdote

Alicia's father was the strictest parent in town, and all her friends knew it. While she wasn't always happy with her dad for being so strict, she realized it did give her an out without losing face among her peers. Her friends all knew when she said, "My dad will kill me if I drink or smoke," it was true. She took comfort in her father's rules.

Discussion

It is important for you to be a role model for your teen. Don't discuss your past party habits in high school. If you do, you are giving your teen the okay sign to drink and to try drugs. You did it in high school, and you still turned out okay, so how bad could it be?! With the current brain research, it is vital that teenagers put drinking and drugs off for as long as possible. The brain is still developing well into one's twenties. Don't be the parent who thinks you need to teach your child how to drink or that allowing your teen to drink in a safe environment is the key. Putting off drinking and drugs for as long as you can is really important. We have so much more information about the effects of drugs and alcohol on the brain now then when we were teenagers.

Advice

- Explain how important it is to delay the use of alcohol and drugs.

- Discuss the dangers of alcohol and drug overuse.

- Discuss the dangers of drinking and driving.

- Set rules and guidelines for your household.

- Discuss the consequences of breaking your household rules.

Example

Tell your teen what your household guidelines are and the consequences. Possible guidelines could be the following: if you partake in drinking alcohol or doing drugs, you will be grounded for a month meaning no cell phone, video games, computer use (except for school use with supervision), driving or having friends over. You will also be drug tested randomly. Include a room search for drug paraphernalia and cell phone search for texts discussing alcohol and drugs. As a parent, you need to decide what you are comfortable with enforcing when house rules are broken. Don't choose rules you are not going to be able to enforce. This sends the wrong message to your teen.

Alcohol/Drug Tests

For alcohol, check your teen's breath by hugging your child to check for the alcohol smell, and notice any issues with balance and speech (slurring). Be sure to test both your teen's urine and hair follicles for possible drug use. Always have a parent present when your teen is taking a urine test. There are ways of fooling the tests like using a friend's urine, or getting a product off the internet for just this purpose. Always research and keep current on these ploys. Staying ahead of teenagers is never easy!

Current Drugs of Choice

Raising teenagers in the internet age has never been harder! New drugs crop up all the time. Research online for the latest drugs of choice and for pictures so you can recognize what the drugs and paraphernalia look like. One place to look for information is The American Council for Drug Education's website: www.acde.org.

Currently, one of the new drugs on the market that is popular in high schools is the drug called "Spice." It is a synthetic form of marijuana that is legal in some states. Spice can be very dangerous depending on what compounds are used to make it. Some people who have used it have experienced seizures, anxiety, increased heart rate, and even death according to Drug Enforcement. Another new drug that has cropped up is called "Bath Salts." It can be snorted, injected, or smoked. Teens and adults who have ingested the drug have become so violent that even police tasers don't subdue them. The drug can be bought at convenience stores and head shops. Recently, the drug has been banned in many states.

Heroin is also a drug of choice for teenagers today because it is cheaper than alcohol and a quicker high. Because the use of heroin has declined among adults, drug traffickers are targeting teenagers, making it easily accessible. It is a highly addictive drug. Molly (Ecstasy) is another popular party drug. Molly is a tablet which is man-made, so it can easily be laced with other drugs making dangerous combinations for your teen.

Other popular drugs are ADHD medications. ADHD medications have been big sellers on high school and college campuses for many years. Students use them to help them study for exams because it helps them focus and stay alert. Teens are able to steal their sibling's supply or sell their own medication. If you have a child who takes ADHD medication, please make sure to secure it properly.

Chapter 4

Parties

"My teenager would NEVER drink or do drugs!"

Anecdote

Elaine had a party in her basement while her parents were upstairs with other chaperones. They checked the teens when they came in to make sure there was no alcohol in their bags or other drug paraphernalia. However, there was a door from the outside to the basement; the teens had stashed alcohol in the bushes and then went outside to get it. A teen who had never tried hard liquor before drank too much and had to be taken to the hospital. Fortunately, one of the teens called 911 instead of trying to handle the situation herself. Many teenagers would have hidden the drunken teen in a closet or taken her up to a bedroom to sleep it off. Both options are very dangerous because she could have choked on her own vomit, or been sexually assaulted, or even died, which happens more often than people realize.

Another fortunate thing about the situation was that several teens made pre-arrangements with their parents so that they would be picked up, no questions asked. Talking to your teen and making plans ahead of time does work!

Discussion

Parents are often afraid to call a host parent whom they don't know to see if adults will be present at the party. They envision a battle with their teen who might say, "It will be so embarrassing if you call. You are the only parent who calls. Why don't you trust me?" Again, this is why it is so important to begin this conversation with your teen early on so it doesn't become a battle, but an expectation. The goal is to put drinking off for as long as you can: DELAY is the key. The current research states that the brain is not fully developed during the teenage years, the frontal lobe is still growing. Alcohol and drugs can hurt brain development, which will affect your teen in later years. Drinking and driving is a problem, but not the only problem where underage drinking or drug use is concerned. Teens can also suffer from alcohol poisoning, date rape, AIDS, sexual assault, brain damage, addiction, and death.

If you do decide to host a party for teenagers, close off all exits, deny car access, and check all bags for alcohol, drug paraphernalia, and prescription drugs. If you are not sure what drug paraphernalia looks like, then check out The American Council for Drug Education's website for information (www.acde.org.) Always ask other parents to help chaperone. Circulate at the party. Don't leave students downstairs by themselves. Check all rooms including the bathroom. Teens may smoke marijuana in the bathroom and try and blow the smoke out the window. Hire an off-duty police officer to be present at the party to ensure proper supervision. If the party gets out of hand and teens from all over begin showing up, call the police. Today's teens can text or tweet about a party, and minutes later large numbers of uninvited teens may show up.

Another good thing to do before you host a teen party is to contact your local police department. Ask if an officer will come to your house to show you potential problems that could occur if you host a party. Also ask for suggestions on how to prevent underage drinking and drug use. The police can also be very helpful if uninvited teenagers show up or if guests arrive intoxicated. Many police departments have a hotline to call where you can leave anonymous information about a drinking party, so it can be broken up before someone gets hurt.

Be aware of your state laws before giving a party for teenagers. The laws are becoming stricter with the blame falling on the host or owner of the house; this includes fines as well as jail time. Know the facts. Explain to your teen that if he or she were to have a party in your absence, and another teen drinks and drives or ends up in the hospital, you are liable. You could lose your house and/or go to jail. Or in an even worse scenario, if a teen dies due to alcohol, you will have to live with that forever.

Advice

- Don't be the parent who wants to be friends with his or her teenager. They have enough friends and don't need another; they need you to be a parent.

- Don't tell your teen about your drug and alcohol use in high school because that tells them it is okay; you did it and look how well you turned out.

- Don't allow your teenager access to your alcohol. Lock the liquor cabinet and any prescription medications.

- Do be the parent who sets guidelines and plans ahead of time about how to deal with parties.

- Even if only one teen has had too much to drink, end the party. Call all the parents to pick up their teens.

- When your teen attends a party, call the parents ahead of time. Ask if they plan to be there along with other adult chaperones, and what are their party policies.

- Make a plan with your teen if drugs or alcohol are brought to the party. Have a code word that means come and pick him or her up.

- Always stay home if your teen is going out, so you can be available if something goes wrong.

- When your teen gets home from a party or other social event, always hug your teen to check for substance use.

- Be sure to tell your teen ahead of time what your family expectations are and what the consequences are for violating those expectations. For example tell your teen if he/she decides to drink or do drugs, he/she will be grounded for a month, which means no weekend activities with friends or driving privileges of any kind.

Know Your State Laws

It is important for parents to be knowledgeable about their state laws regarding underage drinking and parties. Many states have social host liability laws or teen party ordinances. It is important for both you and your teen to understand these laws, so everyone knows what is at risk. For example, in Maryland it is a violation of state law to knowingly and willfully allow possession or consumption of an alcoholic beverage by an underage person. Some state laws say adults who serve or provide alcohol to a person under the age of 21 can be held criminally liable if that minor is killed or injured, or kills or injures another person.

Social Host Liability Laws in some states apply to parents who fail to take adequate precautions to prevent underage drinking on their property; parents can be held liable for negligence. Some laws only hold those adults responsible who knowingly allow underage drinking parties in their home.

Teen Party Ordinances in some states make it illegal to host a party where underage teens are drinking. Under this law, the offence is the hosting of the party itself. Parents and/or siblings can be arrested if they allow a drinking party to occur with their knowledge. Therefore, it is important for parents and teenagers to understand what is at stake if they give a party.

Example

In Maryland, hosting an underage drinking party is punishable by a civil penalty, payable with a fine. Underage persons in possession of alcohol must pay a fine, attend an education course, and perform alternative community service. However, in other states, parents who host such parties can be charged with contributing to the delinquency of a minor, a misdemeanor that can carry jail time.

Brain Research

With all the recent research on the brain, we know the brain is still maturing well into one's twenties. Therefore, allowing teens to drink or do drugs could damage the brain and its ability to function correctly later in life. Also the earlier a teen begins drinking or doing drugs the more likely he or she will become addicted. We all want to give our teens every advantage in life, and clearly early alcohol or drug use puts teens at a disadvantage.

Chapter 5

Friends

"Is it really important to know my teen's friends? I am busy!"

Anecdote

Often parents will tell me they learn more about their teens and their social lives from talking to their teen's friends. It is easier for some teenagers to discuss what is going on in their lives with adults other than their parents. This isn't to say you shouldn't keep trying to talk to your teen, but also try talking to his or her friends.

Discussion

Through middle school and the beginning of high school, teens are trying to determine their identities and find where they fit in. Teens often have changes in friendships, moods, and interests. Some teens want to experiment while others do not. This stage can be very difficult for parents to witness. Try to communicate with your teen and listen. Teenagers can be very unreasonable, and as a parent, this can be hard to navigate.

Advice

- Get to know your teen's friends. Plan an activity that involves you, your teen and his/her friends. You can find out a lot of information from your teen's friends especially if your teen no longer confides in you, which is true for most teenagers.

- Talk to your teen's teachers, coaches, or the other trusted adults in your teen's life. Ask them if they have noticed any changes in your teen.

- Trust your instincts and contact a professional if you and/or others are worried about your teen.

Chapter 6

Driving

"I wish there was a way to keep teenagers off the road!"

Anecdote

Regan drove his intoxicated friends home from a party. A policeman pulled the car over, and although the teenager driving was not intoxicated, the officer soon realized the passengers were. However, only the driver was cited and had to go before a judge and do community service.

Discussion

Driving is a big responsibility. Discuss and plan for all kinds of situations with your teen. Tell your teen how glad you are that he or she is gaining independence, and how proud you are as a parent. Remind him or her also of the risks involved in driving. Ask him or her what situations were discussed in Driver's Ed class. On a separate note, don't buy your teen a sports car. It will only make him or her want to see if it really does go 110 MPH.

If the following situations were not discussed in Driver's Ed, ask your teen about these situations and what he or she would do:

1. What documents do you need when driving?
2. What should you do if a friend asks for a ride, but it will mean you will be home after curfew?
3. What should you do if the friend who was supposed to drive you home, gets drunk?
4. What are the dangers of driving friends who are drunk?
5. What distractions should be eliminated every time you drive?
6. What are the laws about texting and cell phone use while driving?

Advice

Go through the following with your teen and make a plan and discuss consequences:

- Rules for driving others and riding with others.
- Plan for an accident. What to do? Whom to contact?
- Plan for when a rider brings illegal substances into the car.
- Plan for a driver who is drunk.
- Plan for when your teen is unable to drive.
- No headphones while driving.
- No fiddling with the GPS while driving.
- Don't run yellow lights.
- No texting or cell phone use while driving.
- Discuss what it means to be a defensive driver.
- Be sure your teen takes a Driver's Education course.

Chapter 7

Depression

"Aren't all teens supposed to be moody?"

Anecdote

Jansen stopped talking to her parents as most teenagers do in high school. She also quit playing sports and didn't go out much on the weekends anymore. Soon her grades dropped. She spent a lot of time in her bedroom.

Discussion

Once you notice a change in your teen, go with your instincts. Contact teachers and coaches who have daily contact with your teen to see if they have noticed any changes. Do not keep it a secret. Inaction can have dangerous consequences. Seek professional advice if you are truly worried. Often tension exists between teens and parents, so utilize the school personnel to act as a go between or to be your eyes.

Signs of Depression

The following are signs of depression: mood changes, loss of interest in hobbies, low energy, loner behavior, difficulty getting out of bed and going to school, feelings of being overwhelmed, changes in eating patterns, changes in affect or appearance, personality change, change in peer groups, cutting, or grades dropping.

Advice

- Listen to your instincts and look for signs that something may be wrong.

- Seek help from your teen's school.

- Contact your teen's advisor, coach, counselor, Dean of Students or Principal.

- If after consulting with the school counselor, you feel you need outside help, contact a psychiatrist or psychologist. There are also treatment programs and support groups for teenagers.

- Remember that teenagers often lie under difficult circumstances. This is especially true if they have a drug problem. Drugs often mask the depression. Teenagers sometimes lie because they don't want to disappoint you, or they do not want to get in trouble. Keep the lines of communication open and do not be naïve and insist that your teen could not possibly have done something wrong.

- The frontal lobe of the teenage brain is not fully developed which causes them to make poor decisions. Depression compounds the poor decision-making.

Chapter 8

Sex

"Who wants to discuss sex with a teenager?"

Anecdote

Jane had a boyfriend for the first time. She liked the attention he gave her, but wasn't sure how she felt about him and sex. Her parents had never had a conversation with her about sex, and she didn't know how to bring the subject up with her parents.

Discussion

No one wants to discuss sex; that is the problem. It is important for you to have a talk with your teen before he/she experiences sex. Let him/her know it is not okay to have oral sex or to "hook up" as they call it. This is demeaning and void of emotion or commitment. Many teens believe that oral sex is okay. They don't realize they can get STDs from oral sex. They also don't realize the emotional impact of having these encounters with one another without a relationship. Teens are not learning how to interact with one another in a caring relationship. Many boys are never being told no, and as a result, they are not learning how to respect women. And both genders are not learning how to love and be in a committed relationship.

Advice

Discuss with your teen what kind of sex (if any at all) is appropriate or inappropriate at his or her age. Make a plan with your teen for what to do if a date goes wrong. Talk to your teen about a loving relationship you had as teenager. Your first love doesn't necessarily mean the first time you had sex. Make sure your teen knows that no one should be pressured into sex. Be sure your teen knows sex doesn't equal love. Even if their friends are having sex, it doesn't mean they should. It is important for your teen to know what to say or how to handle situations that make him or her uncomfortable. If your family is part of a faith-based tradition, be sure to frame the conversation around the moral teachings of your religion and your family values.

Chapter 9

Sports/Activities

"Aren't academics more important?"

Anecdote

Mark is not involved in any school activities or sports. He spends all of his free time on the computer and has become addicted to certain games. He has also gained weight due to inactivity.

Discussion

Students who are not involved in activities in school, tend to find their own type of activities which are not usually healthy. Also, if they hang out with friends after school who also are not involved in extracurriculars, they tend to experiment with drugs and alcohol. Teens need outlets besides academics. All work and no play is not healthy. Teens need physical activity for both their minds and bodies. This helps with creativity both now and later in life. With technology changing our world and the way we do things, this generation especially needs to be more active and creative.

Advice

It is important for your teen to be involved in some activity in high school, not only because it makes your teen connected to his or her school, but also because it allows your teen to discover other interests. Colleges also want to see that your teen is well-rounded and has pursuits other than academics. However, the most important reason to join a club or sport is because your teen has a strong interest in that area. It is important for your teen to be passionate about what he or she does. Joining a lot of clubs and participating in a lot of sports is not ideal. It is more important for your teen to find one or two activities he or she feels strongly about and really pursue them. This is what colleges are after, not someone who has joined a myriad of clubs but hasn't really gained anything from them.

Another benefit of activities is that coaches and club leaders can be good role models for your teen. Also the social aspect of interacting with other teens is important. The following are other reasons your teen should be involved:

- Social and physical benefits
- Productive time use prevents poor choices
- Sports are a deterrent to substance abuse
- A healthy extracurricular list improves chances for college admission
- Teens learn how to work with all types of people
- Activities increase bonds with friends
- Sports are a life-long healthy habit

If your teen is not interested in competitive team sports, try other activities such as karate, music or dance.

Chapter 10

Internet Issues

"I can barely handle keeping up with all the Facebook settings, so how am I going to tell what my teen is doing on the computer!"

Anecdote

On the wall of Joe's Facebook page, several of his friends had discussions with people none of them knew. They didn't think twice about it because it was the wall of a friend. Unknowingly, they gave a complete stranger their names and the name of their school. This person was an adult and could easily access these students if he wanted to.

Discussion

Teens think the internet is safe and Facebook even safer because it has privacy settings. Teens don't think someone they don't know will be able to access their information. They truly don't understand the risks, and they don't think about how the pictures they post or the witty repartee they have with their friends will be taken or received by others. Teens often text, tweet, and post items without a thought. Helping your teen understand the dangers of their words and pictures is important. A teen's reputation can be damaged in seconds on the internet and made accessible for all to see. Teens often think they can just delete items before they apply to college or for jobs. However, there is a website called archive.org which contains deleted items. Colleges, universities, and employers check potential students or employees' Facebook pages before accepting or hiring them. Also campus police on university campuses use Facebook to find out where the parties are to bust underage drinking.

Advice

- Go over the dangers with your teen.

- Tell them to be safe – don't put personal information on the internet.

- Tell them to be respectful – think before you send.

- Tell them to report inappropriate or offensive communication to an adult.

- Be sure your teen knows that behavior which is disrespectful of others is inappropriate and unacceptable. This includes the following: bullying, intimidation, derogatory statements, discriminatory comments, obscene communication, spreading false rumors or accusations, demeaning jokes or comments, name-calling, and comments that offend another.

Encourage your teen to come to you if there is a problem. Monitor your teen's internet use. Also check your teen's cell phone for unknown numbers or texts. Be sure your teen uses his/her computer in a common area and not in his/her bedroom. Check your teen's Facebook page to make sure pictures are appropriate and no personal contact information is provided. Inform your teen that colleges and jobs check Facebook and other sites for inappropriate images, etc. Check your teen's privacy settings on all social websites where he or she posts pictures and information. Currently, Facebook is under fire in Germany for automatically storing pictures and information on its users. There is a setting a user can select so they won't do this, but the argument is that it should be the other way around. The company should only archive information if they are given permission to do so.

Examples of Inappropriate Internet Use

- Sending threats to another through email, texts or blogs
- Racist remarks transmitted via email, texts or blogs
- Downloading pornography
- Sending inappropriate pictures of friends
- Setting up an "I hate teacher X" club on Facebook

New Trends

The internet keeps parents and adults who work with teens a step behind. Even Facebook is becoming passé; teens are turning to other social websites because Facebook is not "cool enough" anymore. Since most parents are on Facebook now, teens are looking for alternative social media such as Pinterest, Instagram, Tumblr, Snapchat and Yik Yak. Keeping up with the new websites can be a challenge!

Chapter 11

Time Management

"When does my teen get to breathe?"

Anecdote

Robin wants to go to the movies at midnight yet leaves the house at 9:00 p.m. She asks for money before leaving. Her parents never ask any questions such as: Who are you going with? What are you going to do for 3 hours? When are you going to get your homework done? The next day Robin goes to school and has done no homework and is too tired to participate in her after school activities. This not only hurts her grades but also her reputation and her ability to commit.

Discussion

Choosing an appropriate balance between academics, athletics, and extracurricular commitments both inside and outside of school is a real skill. It is one your teen will need to have mastered to do well in high school, college, and even later in life.

First discuss with your teen what sports and activities he/she wants to be involved in and how he/she plans to manage it all with his/her academic schedule. Can they make a true commitment to each of these activities and do a good job? It is not fair to their peers, teachers, sponsors or coaches to not fully commit. How will they ensure balance?

Have your teen plan out each week's events including social events, so he/she can see when things can be done. Your teen should have a clear plan for each day including 10 to 15 minutes to study for test a few days away. Your teen can even include TV shows in the plan so he/she will see exactly how the time will be spent to get things done efficiently and effectively. See Appendix A (page 103) for a sample One-Week Study Schedule.

Advice

Make sure your teen has a place to study in a common area with few distractions. Have your teen's plan for each week clearly visible so your teen will know exactly what he/she needs to do each day. Encourage your child to communicate when he/she has overextended himself or herself. Be upfront and honest with those involved. Your teen needs to advocate for himself or herself. Sleep is also very important. Make sure your teen gets enough sleep. So many other problems crop up if your teen doesn't get enough sleep. Sleep deprivation can make him or her more emotional and not handle situations well. Your teen's memory and health can also be affected.

Chapter 12

Tutoring

*"I can get the tutor to do my teen's homework!
Problem solved!"*

Anecdote

Ricky's parents had demanding jobs and didn't have the time to spend checking Ricky's assignments, so they decided to hire a tutor for every subject. While Ricky's grades improved, he could not function without the tutors. While the tutors were a band-aid solution, it was not a long-term way to help Ricky learn to handle his academic strengths and weaknesses.

Discussion

Before hiring a tutor, make sure your teen has exhausted all other avenues. You don't want your teen to become dependent on a tutor. The key is for your teen to self-advocate and figure out what he/she doesn't know or understand. Has your teen truly applied himself or herself and spent time trying to learn the material? Has your teen taken what she/he doesn't understand to the teacher for help? If your teen needs extensive help beyond meeting with the teacher for a few extra help sessions, then hire a tutor. Don't be the parent that hires a tutor for every subject. This just overwhelms your teen and gives him/her no independence. Students need to learn how to handle down time especially before they go off to college. Teens need to learn to work on their own. Organization is a valuable tool for a teen to have to both get out of high school and in to college. There is also a self-esteem piece that goes along with being able to handle and control one's own life. Parents need to equip their teens with tools to succeed, not hinder their growth and make them feel useless.

Advice

If your teen is having trouble in school, meet with his/her teachers and academic administrators and make a plan to help support your teen. If your teen has really made an effort to meet with teachers, discuss the idea of hiring a tutor with advice from your teen's teachers, advisor, or academic administrator.

Plan out the week – which teachers do I need to see? When will I see them? What is my sports schedule like? Do I have any social commitments? See Appendix A (page 103) for a Sample One-Week Study Schedule.

Chapter 13

Partnering with Your School

"Do educators really have time for parents?"

Anecdote

Juliana became very moody. Her mother was worried and didn't know what to do. Was Juliana moody because all teens are moody? Was she depressed? Since this was the first teenager in the house, the parents were at a loss.

Discussion

Schools want to work together with the parents to ensure all teens have a good high school experience. It is very important to have a relationship with your teen's school. You should know the important people in your teen's life. Check in with the people with whom your teen spends most of his/her time such as a coach, advisor, or teacher. Schools have counselors that are available as well.

Advice

- Take a team approach – not parents versus school. Educators are there to help, not hinder.

- Let the school know if you will be away, if there is a lifestyle change (divorce, new baby, tragedy).

- If you are worried your teen is acting differently, get advice from the school on ways to handle it.

- Is your teen handling the increased pressure of high school?

- Is your teen involved in too many activities? Or not involved enough?

Schools can help in a number of ways. Don't be afraid to contact administrators, counselors, advisors, coaches, or teachers. If other professionals are needed, the school can give you referrals. Don't wait until your child is in crisis to seek advice. With the ever-increasing pressure to get into the right college, high school can be daunting for many. Work as a team with your school to ensure the best possible experience for your teen.

Chapter 14

Parenting

"Will I really survive the teenage years?"

Anecdote

Jack was very different from his older brother Jason. Yet, his parents treated him the same. Jack felt like he continually disappointed his parents. This made him unhappy and unable to connect with his parents. They argued all the time. Jack's parents never seemed to listen.

Discussion

The big mistake most parents make is not listening to their teen. Try to see your teen for whom he/she is. Get to know your teen's friends and their parents. Go to school events. Meet your teens teachers and coaches. Conversation is key. Think through the rules and guidelines for your child. What is important to you and what are your family values? Have you effectively conveyed this to your teen? Discuss the ideal situation and what to do when things go wrong. Think about the following questions when your teen is in middle school: When will you let your child go to parties? Can your child drive with another teenager? How much computer/game use will you allow?

When your child was a baby, the main concerns were eating, sleeping, and baby-proofing the house. Now you must teenage-proof your teen's world. The teenage years are not the time to do less parenting – they need you! Let them be independent, but make sure you have equipped them with the proper tools. Let them fail, just as you let them stumble when they were toddlers, but be there to help them get back on their feet.

Advice

More is more…be involved.

- Listen to your teen.

- Talk to and get to know your child's friends (have them over for dinner, take them to the movies/miniature golfing, etc.)

- Set time aside once a week for a family walk, TV show, outing, movie, bowling—to allow conversations to happen and give your full attention. This is an "e-free" evening with no cell phones. Make sure it is an activity that kids will enjoy.

- Boundaries and rules are critical. Even though you want to be the cool parent, deep down inside they really want you to protect them. Be their excuse, "My dad will freak out if I come home drunk."

Part Two:
Getting in to College

This section of the book focuses on the details of the college application process, and it offers insights about managing the stressful aspects of the college search.

Chapter 15

Top 10 Mistakes Parents Make and How to Fix Them

"Now what the heck do I do?"

Top 10 Mistakes Parents Make During the College Process and How to Fix Them

1. **Starting the process too late.** Begin researching colleges sophomore year.

2. **Letting the gossip on the "cocktail circuit" determine where your teen applies.** Use guidebooks, not gossip, to inform your decision.

3. **Allowing your ego to affect the list of colleges your teen selects.** Remember: it's not about you this time.

4. **Avoiding the topic of college because it is too stressful.** Limit dialogue to one night a week at dinner or at a family meeting time.

5. **Writing your teen's essay or application for him or her.** Colleges compare the writing from the essays on standardized tests to see if it matches the writing on the application.

6. **Leaving visits to senior year after your teen has been accepted.** Start visiting junior year during spring break.

7. **Not being realistic about what your family can afford.** Research tuition costs well before you apply.

8. **Not writing a parent recommendation letter to your college counselor to provide extra information about your teen.** Submit this the summer before senior year.

9. **Not allowing your teen to choose which college he/she wants to attend.** Letting your teen choose now could prevent the hassle of a transfer later.

10. **Asking your teen's teachers for recommendations rather than letting him/her ask.** How can a teacher write about independence and maturity if you are still doing everything for your teen?

Chapter 16

How to Research Colleges

"Going beyond gossip and Facebook"

- How do you begin your research about colleges? Go to the library or bookstore and get a copy of the college guidance books. *The Fiske Guide* is an excellent source of helpful information about deadlines, college facts, testing score ranges, etc. Balance this reading with *The Insider's Guide to the Colleges*, a book written by students, for students. This gives you the "dirt" on colleges. Is this a party school? Does everyone leave campus on the weekends making it a "suitcase school"? Is it hard to get into the classes you want to take? Is safety an issue on campus?

- Use the college websites...often their virtual tours are a great way to introduce yourself to the campus. Check out any blogs by students...even admissions officers jump on these from time to time to answer questions.

- Use your college counseling office's tracking software such as Naviance to see a scattergram of where students from your high school with similar profiles were accepted.

- Read the online college newspaper. This will give you a glimpse into what is making news on campus, both good and bad.

- Meet with admissions officers when they visit your school. Not only will you garner information about the college, but you will make the all-important personal connection or "contact."

- Speak with current students and alumni who may live in your area. Anecdotal evidence from students who actually attended the college can really help give you a picture of campus life.

- Set up an alumni interview. These interviewers are trained to field questions about their alma mater. Plus the interview could enhance your chances of admission!

Chapter 17

How to Prepare for the Interview

"Can he really wear that?"

- Practice answering questions in front of the mirror. It may sound silly, but looking at yourself in the mirror is a great distraction. It forces you to think through your answers, and it enables you to hear how your responses truly sound. It is one thing to read over a list of interview questions, but it is quite another to say the answers out loud. (You will find a list of sample interview questions in Chapter 18 on page 63.)

- Visit the college's website before the interview. Read about the academic offerings so that you are prepared for the question often asked by interviewers, "Do you have any questions about our college?" or "Why do you want to attend our college?" It is important that you do not ask a question such as, "Tell me more about your nursing program" if the college does not have a nursing program. This shows you did not do your research and are not really serious about the college.

- Practice driving the route to the interview location a few days before your scheduled meeting to ensure that you have clear directions. On the day of the interview, allow plenty of time to find parking and to deal with traffic. Try on your interview clothes a few days before to ensure that everything fits and there are no holes or rips. Put everything you need for the interview by the door the night before. This includes directions, breath mints, a water bottle and a copy of your resume.

- If a college recommends an interview, be sure to sign up for this early in the application process. If a college representative is coming to visit your school, he or she may be available to interview you while he or she is in town. Check well-ahead of the representative's visit to see if this is an option. Your college counseling office will have the official visit schedule.

- Other colleges offer Skype interviews. In this case, be sure to test your Skype connection ahead of time and ensure that you have a quiet place to conduct the interview.

Chapter 18

Common Interview Questions

"Like, Whatever, Dude"

Colleges often ask their interviewers to focus on those aspects of an applicant which they cannot learn from just reading an application. Surprisingly, most questions do not focus on grades, but on things *outside* of the classroom. The interviewers are trying to learn more about the applicant as a person. Here are some sample questions:

1. Tell me about your family.

2. What is your favorite class in school and why?

3. Why do you want to attend our college? (This is a critical question. The interviewer wants to hear that you are genuinely interested in the college and have done your research.) Do not say, *"Because I am looking for a small liberal arts college with nice weather or ski slopes or the beach nearby!"*

4. What do you think is a major issue facing the US today?

5. What did you do last summer? (Can you believe they still ask that?!)

6. How would your friends describe you?

7. Tell me about your most meaningful extracurricular activity.

Hints:

- DO dress nicely...no jeans or gym shorts.

- DO arrive on time...a few minutes early is even better.

- DO send a thank you email or note post interview.

- DO understand that the interviewer is a regular person interested in learning more about you.

- DO try to relax...you will be more yourself.

Chapter 19

Testing

"Does it really matter?"

- **Should Your Teen Take the SAT or the ACT?** Many years ago, only Midwestern colleges accepted the ACT. Today nearly all colleges accept it. The main differences between the two standardized tests are that the ACT includes a science component, and it does not penalize for incorrect answers. Some students find the wording of the ACT questions more straightforward than the SAT, and thus score higher on that particular test. However, students should take both the SAT and ACT in the spring of their junior year, and then retake the test on which they scored higher. Another approach is to have your teen visit the test websites, try their free practice test questions online, and determine which test seems more suited to his or her strengths. Finally, some test preparation centers offer an evaluation tool that can help students determine which test they will score higher on before they register for the tests. At press time, the SAT was gearing up to revise their test, so be sure to read about the most current changes on their website (www.collegeboard.com.)

- **When Should Your Teen Take the Tests?** Your teen should take the test during the spring of junior year...the specific date might be determined by your teen's extracurricular and social schedule. In reality, testing the day of the Big Game or the Big Dance can be a huge distraction, so try to avoid these dates. After receiving the scores, determine which specific areas your student needs to focus on improving. Be sure to examine the online score report for the SAT which shows the student's answer, the correct answer, and the degree of difficulty for each question. This allows your teen to target future preparation.

- **How to Prepare: Class, Tutor or Self?** This is directly related to the learning style and personality of your teen. Is he or she self-motivated and extremely busy? Would fitting in a class once a week be next to impossible? If so, get a book from the bookstore and set your own schedule or prepare for the test with online resources. Or does your teen need the routine of a regularly scheduled class to get things accomplished? Ask other parents and your school's college counseling office for reputable programs. Finally, a private tutor is the appropriate choice if your student performs better with one-on-one teaching. A private tutor can often target the specific areas which your teen needs to improve. For example, if your teen did well on the math section, why spend time in a class learning math when you could be focusing solely on the subject area of weakness?

- **What if Your Teen is a Poor Tester?** More and more colleges are steering away from standardized testing as a factor in determining admission. Go to www.Fairtest.org for a complete list of colleges which do not require standardized testing. The list includes several top tier colleges. Simply scanning the alphabetical list will reveal such well-respected colleges as Bard, Bates, Bowdoin and Connecticut College. (This is just a sampling of the first letters of the alphabet.) Also, if testing is not your student's forté, be sure to emphasize other areas that are strengths. Consider sending a paragraph along with the applications explaining that while your student is not a strong tester, he/she has demonstrated hard work in the classroom, or boasts the following achievements in art, sports, etc. Colleges appreciate it when students acknowledge weaknesses as it shows self-awareness, a sure sign of maturity.

- **When Should Your Teenager Register for the Test?** Whichever test you choose, register early. The longer you wait to register, the chances of taking the test at a school close to you decreases. If your local test center is full, you risk being sent to a test center which is far away. There is nothing worse than getting up EVEN earlier on the big day and driving further away than would have been necessary had you registered early. However, if this happens to you, take a practice drive several days before the test to ensure you know the route and are not surprised by road closures, construction, etc.

- **How Do You Receive Extended Time on the Standardized Tests?** This is a critical point: you must start the paperwork early with the ACT and SAT if you hope to qualify for extended time on the testing day. A learning difference documented by a psychologist must be in place for this accommodation. It can take months to get the paperwork through. Be sure to let your high school guidance office know that you qualify for extended time in the fall of your junior year, and learn what steps are necessary on your end. Usually, you need to use extended time currently in the classroom to receive it on standardized tests.

- **Should I Send All of My Scores to Colleges?** If you use the score choice feature with the SAT, you can decide which scores the colleges will see. The downside of this option is that it costs around $11.00 to send scores to each college. The upside is that you are in control of which scores the colleges see. Most colleges take the highest scores from any test date; this is called "superscoring." The ACT only sends scores to colleges according to which scores you select. Standardized test companies often change their policies, so check their websites for the most up-to-date changes to policies. Please note that there are a handful of colleges which require that you send all test scores as part of your application.

Chapter 20

Finding a Good Fit

"College talk and cocktails don't mix"

- It will be virtually impossible to do anything socially junior or senior year with parents of college-bound students without hearing the dreaded, "Where is junior applying?" It is best to prepare yourself for this insensitive barrage into your business with a few pat responses. Be sure to have your "hurt feelings" shield up as certainly you will encounter a parent who makes you and/or your teen feel inferior due to the list of colleges you have selected. Don't let the raised eyebrows or condescending remarks such as, "Oh, that's an *interesting* choice!" or "Oh yes, X University is our safety school!" rattle you or influence your decision. Research is the most reliable source of information about colleges, not rumors or other parents.

- Would you let your peers pick out your future spouse or your future home? Of course not—this is a personal decision. So you should follow the same philosophy for choosing a college—after all, the financial investment will be as substantial as a home! Do your homework and decide what is best for you.

- It is better to go for a good fit with a college, rather than a brand name. What good is that name going to do you if the college does not suit the student? Then you end up with a transfer on your hands which means you get to do the process *all over again.* Consider what you have taught your teen: "Don't fall for peer pressure. Make your own wise decisions." So why would you yourself fall for parental peer pressure?

- Bragging rights are much less important in the long run than a happy teen. Imagine if you force your student to go to the college *you* want him/her to attend and he/she ends up unhappy there. Some students even sabotage their grades to "get back" at mom and dad and do the ultimate I-told-you-so while others may call crying from college because they feel out of place.

- Avoid both of these scenarios by communicating with your teen from the start. How exactly do you communicate with a teenager? How are you supposed to calmly discuss BIG LIFE issues like college when you cannot even calmly discuss why junior must take the garbage out? Well, this is where a third party can be very helpful. Enlist the help of your school's college counselor or hire a private counselor. Both will know how to navigate the process and can serve as a communication facilitator for you. And, the mere presence of a third party prevents emotionally-charged discussions from eroding into parent/teen arguments.

Chapter 21

Tips for Visiting College Campuses

"Looking beyond the cute tour guide"

When visiting campuses, you must go beyond the "dog and pony show" offered by the Admissions Office. The students featured in their presentations are carefully selected and well-trained as they are the "face" of the campus. It is up to you to investigate the college on your own. You want to learn *now* what issues may plague the campus, not after your teen has committed to attending the college. These tips below will tell you how to look beyond the Admissions' presentation to get a complete picture of the college.

- Have a coffee in the cafeteria so you get a sense of what the students are like (purple hair, tattooed all over, etc—these might be good or bad in your opinion.) Get up the nerve to ask a current student one thing the college does right and one thing that needs improvement.

- Pick up a college newspaper as it reveals the issues the students are fired up about, but the Admissions Office is not mentioning. In particular, look for campus safety issues or registration issues (i.e. all the "good classes" filling up or freshmen not getting into certain classes.)

- Try to meet one professor in the academic department in which your teen is interested. Get his or her card to email questions which may arise later. This conversation can also add specificity to your teen's response to the "Why Do You Want to Attend Our University?" question on the application.

- Use the same approach if you meet a college student involved in student government, theater, community service, sports (or whatever your "thing" is.)

- Sign in at the Admissions Office. This serves as your official visit to the campus and enhances your application (as demonstrated interest or a "contact.") If the office is closed, send an email after your visit asking Admissions to note in your file that you were on campus. Many colleges keep a record of contacts; they use this factor in determining your interest level.

- Consider taking a separate tour from your teen. This way you can compare tour guides and evaluate answers to different questions that arose from your group. This also allows for parents and teenagers to ask questions which they might not ask if the other party were present. It also provides a bit of much needed space from the "together time" that these long trips involve.

- Visit the Financial Aid Office; it's never too early to plan.

- Keep a journal with notes about your visit; this will be invaluable when all the campuses blend together in your head. Use your journal notes to write your response to "Why do you want to attend our university?"

- Pick up an application while you are visiting. You can read these applications while traveling and brainstorm about the answers to the short answer questions.

- Try to enjoy the time together on this trip. See a few sights to break up the campus clutter in your mind.

- Consult alternative resources. Check out the latest apps for college visits. Get a copy of the Princeton Review's *Visiting College Campuses*. This book includes directions to other colleges nearby, admissions' office hours, local restaurant and hotel information, etc. Also, utilize AAA for trip-tiks mapping the most efficient route between colleges or try Google Maps.

Chapter 22

Application Tips

"Crayon is a no-no"

- Be honest. If you are caught in a lie, admission will be denied and colleges share that information with one another.

- Invest as much time in the short answer questions as you did on your essay. Many colleges pay closer attention to the writing here because they know you probably had help with your essay, but not with the short answers, so these responses accurately reflect your writing.

- Write a resume. It is a useful brainstorming tool for essay topics, and is a good "cheat sheet" to look at in the waiting room before an interview. Be sure to include activities outside of school such as in a religious organization or in your community. List all jobs including babysitting and volunteer positions.

- Do not use an inappropriate or bizarre email address on your application. This does not put forth the image you are trying to project.

- Be sure your application is error-free. Have someone else proofread for errors as well.

Chapter 23

Contacts with Colleges

"Is Kindergarten too early to start your college search?"

Is a tour enough to demonstrate interest in a college? No. Contacts are critical in this process; they are how colleges gauge who is going to accept their acceptance. This plays into their yield, a key factor in determining their rankings in *US News and World Report*. So, no, a tour is not enough to demonstrate interest.

Students should create a stream of contacts. Here are some options:

- Write a thank you note or email to the interviewer after an interview.
- Send a quick email after a visit saying how terrific your experience on campus was.
- Submit a question to admissions via email or phone. (Make sure the answer isn't readily apparent on the website.)
- Sign the contact card when the admissions representative comes to your school. Representatives do not look kindly on students who do not bother to say hello during the representative's visit to their high school. If your teen has a test or cannot miss class, he or she

should say hello to the representative, explain why he/she cannot stay, and most importantly, fill out a contact card before leaving.

- At college fairs, be sure to check off the contact sheet which is often provided. (Bringing a list of pre-printed address labels will save you time here.)

All of these types of correspondence count as contacts. None of these take much time, yet they can make the difference between an acceptance and a denial, particularly at the smaller, private colleges. Many of the larger, state schools do not consider contacts as part of their evaluation because it is not feasible due to the large volume of applicants.

Chapter 24

Troubleshooting

"The %ˆ&# Chapter"

Read on to see what to do if things do not go as planned...

- It's senior year and you haven't visited anywhere...what should you do? Get out the school calendar and look for a few test-free days to take off from school. Plan to visit local colleges on Saturdays or half-days. Save longer drives or flights for long weekends. Although visiting a college campus is important in terms of demonstrating interest, you can also apply to colleges, see where you are accepted, and then use the month of April senior year to visit one or two colleges. The downside to this approach is that the time box of April may make the decision more pressure-filled. (Students must commit to a college by May 1st.)

- You have had a significant change in your financial situation due to losing a job or a spouse. In this case, call the Financial Aid office at the college your teen is slated to attend to discuss options. Most colleges will be understanding and try to think of creative solutions with you.

- Your teen is miserable at college and wants to transfer. First, give your teen time to adjust. This may be a case of homesickness which will improve in a few weeks or a few months. If your teen still wants to transfer, make sure he or she continues to do well in classes as the next college will want a letter of good academic standing as well as a recommendation from a current professor.

- Your activity section is light and could use a boost. Use the summer. Students should not make the mistake of lounging on the beach or by the pool all summer. Yes, summer is a time for relaxation, but the infamous question, "What did you do last summer?" pops up on applications and in interviews all the time. Students should find a balance: perhaps work two days a week and play the other five. They might offer their services without pay as an intern to a local newspaper, a business, or a community service organization.

Another option is a paying job. Colleges respect the fact that students are reliable enough to hold a job. And, as a bonus, their employer just might be able to write them a glowing recommendation! Babysitting and lifeguarding are excellent job choices as the colleges reason that if someone trusts a student with their kid's safety, they must be responsible. The best bet for a summer experience is one that plays into a student's interests. For example, if a student wants to be a veterinarian, he or she could volunteer or work at a local shelter. Colleges like to see that a student has already "tried out" his or her intended profession.

- Your teen is not ready for college and needs to wait a year. Most colleges allow students to defer, which means they will hold a spot for the student in next year's class. Your teen could use the time to work or try a gap year program. These programs range from international service trips to outdoor adventures. Check with your college counseling office for programs.

Chapter 25

The Common Application

"Isn't 'common' the last thing you want on an application?"

- **The Application Itself.** The Common Application is widely accepted today. Students use this one application to apply to many colleges. The application itself includes biographical information, test scores, coursework, activities and honors. There is one short answer question about a significant extracurricular activity and one essay. Every August the Common Application rolls out a revised application, so be sure to use the most current edition.

- **Supplements.** Most colleges require supplements for the Common Application. Some supplements are merely a page with a few brief questions, while other supplements have several short answers or even more essays. The short answers on the application are critical! Colleges know the student has spent a great deal of time on the essay and perhaps had many eyes look over it. However, the short answers provide a truer representation of the student's writing, so colleges look closely at these. A short answer response is typically 150 words, which is about a paragraph. Students should make their response concise but well-constructed.

- **Applying Online.** Today nearly all colleges prefer receiving online applications. This entails creating an account and completing the application online. Type your essay and short answer responses in a Word document, use spellcheck, then cut and paste or upload into the online application. Students should print out their application before hitting "submit" to make sure that no responses are truncated, and that there are no errors or omissions. Parents should proofread the student's application before submission. If a student encounters a problem, technical assistance via email is available for the Common Application as well as for many other college applications.

- **Timing.** The summer before senior year is the best time to fill out applications. Students who take advantage of this block of time begin senior year ahead of the game and less stressed. It is very difficult to balance school work with the time-consuming task of completing applications.

- **Website.** Visit www.commonapp.org for a complete list of colleges which accept the common application. You will find links to college websites as well as links to the school-specific supplements.

- There is another application which is used by several colleges called the Universal Application. Visit www. universalcollegeapp.com to read more about this option.

Chapter 26

The Essay

"The Good, the Bad and the Ugly"

- Does it matter what topic your student chooses for his or her essay? YES! The essay is the only opportunity in the application for students to let their personalities shine through. Students should take reasonable risks. If he/she is a humorous writer, he/she should try writing a funny but thoughtful piece. The best essays speak from the student's heart and reveal where his or her passion lies.

- The essay is perhaps the most critical part of the application. Of course, grades, test scores and teacher recommendations are important, but the essay is the aspect of the application over which students have total control. It is important for students to allow their own voice to come through in the essay. Students can have someone edit their essay, but not rewrite it. The topic choice is the critical part of writing the essay. Without a good topic, students will lose interest in their own subject, and certainly the admissions officer reading their essay will as well.

- What should students write about? They should write about whatever is most important to them in their life.

Nowadays, most colleges allow a free choice topic, so it is likely that students will be able to write on what matters to them. If a student writes on a subject that he or she is passionate about, it will come through in their writing.

• Should a student try to be funny in the essay? If he/she is a humorous writer—this means someone else like a teacher has told him or her that he/she is funny—then he/she should go for it. If a student thinks he or she is a humorous writer but has never been recognized as such, this is not the time to experiment. Should a student opt for the humorous route—taking risks is key. For example, one successful essay was on McDonald's Big Mac, a topic a student's parents were strongly opposed to, but which ultimately ended in admission. Another great essay was on the importance of duct tape over a student's high school career from reaffixing a tuxedo button at a dance to holding together Homecoming floats. The student even attached a piece of duct tape to the essay. Again, admission was granted.

• Should students include a picture? Yes, if they have one that is in focus and adds meaning to their essay. For example, one student attached a picture of his family holding a rubber turkey to illustrate the annual Turkey Bowl game that his family played at Thanksgiving. A picture personalizes the essay. It can grab the admissions officer's attention and help him or her remember the essay. Many online applications offer options to upload a picture.

• Should students write about someone who has influenced

them? This topic is very difficult to execute because often the essay tells more about the other person than the applicant. This defeats the purpose of the essay. If the essay describes a lesson learned from the influential person and reveals how that lesson stays with him or her today, it can work.

- Should students write about community service? Community service is an admirable thing, and colleges do like to know that a student has dedicated his/her time to helping others. However, students frequently write about this topic, so it is best to write about community service in two situations: 1. If a student has done an extraordinary amount of community service, well beyond what their school requires, or 2. If the student can write about his or her service in an unusual way as illustrated in the example below.

Example: A student wanted to write her essay on the service trip she took to the Bahamas. She was honest in the opening paragraph explaining that she went on the trip to get tan and party. However, once there she realized the only tan she would be getting was a "farmer's tan" from working in the fields in shorts all day (instead of on the beach in a swimsuit), and that she had no energy to party at night after the rigorous physical labor all day. Of course, the essay goes on to discuss lessons learned, and it handles the subject in an honest, innovative manner.

- Should students write about a death in the family? This is an appropriate decision only if the death has had a tremendous impact on their life.

- How does a student get started on the essay? Students should begin by brainstorming topics and answering the question, "What matters to me?" with three different responses. Then students write "trial" paragraphs on each of the three topics. It doesn't matter if it is an introductory paragraph, a body paragraph or a conclusion…the point is to "test drive" the topic to see if it "has wheels." By doing this exercise, students will see which topic peters out after a paragraph, or which topic leaves the student uncertain of where he/she is going with the essay, or which topic gets the student inspired to write more.

- How long should the essay be? The essay length should adhere to the word limit, usually this is 500 to 750 words. (At press time, the Common Application limits essays to 650 words.) Students must remember that admissions officers are reading *hundreds* of essays. Their essay should be concise and impactful, with any unnecessary parts trimmed. This is where it can be helpful to have a friend read the essay to determine which parts are worth keeping.

Chapter 27

Recommendations

"I need somebody to love me"

- Whom should a student ask for a recommendation? This question is often answered by looking at the actual college application. Some colleges are intent on having the letter written by a junior year teacher, others insist on a "core subject" teacher such as math or English.

- If there are no guidelines from the college as to who should write the letter, students should go with their gut feeling, asking themselves: "Who knows me the best? Who would be able to give specific examples of my academic ability or work ethic?" It does not necessarily have to be a teacher from a class for which the student earned a high grade...working hard in the class can be impactful. When in doubt, students should ask the teacher if he/she feels comfortable writing them a strong letter.

- Students must check with their school's college counseling office as to the policy of asking more than one teacher to write letters on their behalf.

- When should students ask the teacher? Students should ask in the spring of junior year if possible. Some teachers put a limit on the number of recommendation letters that they will write. Students don't want to learn about that limit when it is too late. Also, many teachers write their recommendations during the summer, so asking in the fall of senior year could be too late.

- Should students have their Congressperson/dignitary/important person write a letter on their behalf? Only if that person knows the applicant well. Admissions officers like to joke about getting letters from well-known people that say, "Although I have never actually met Joey, I hear he is a really great kid!"

- Should students have a non-teacher write them a letter? Letters from coaches, dance teachers, Model UN supervisors, etc. are appropriate *only* if they will significantly add to the application. Students risk appearing as though they are "padding the application" with extra letters to make up for a lack of substance in their overall application. A wiser approach is for students to ask the person to submit a quote to their college counseling office for inclusion in the letter that school will write on their behalf to the colleges. (Often a person might balk at the idea of having to write a whole recommendation letter, but a single quote is very doable.)

- What role does being a legacy have in the process? This varies by college. Some colleges mark an application "Special Interest Student" for legacies, thus giving the applicant an edge in the process. Other colleges only count students as legacies if both parents are alumni. It is best for the student to contact admissions to ask how the process is handled.

Chapter 28

Artists, Athletes and Actors

"My Talented Teen"

- Artists should be sure to check the college's instructions for portfolios. They should not assume that one portfolio will work for all colleges. Artists should take advantage of Portfolio Days when colleges come to the area to examine portfolios. Some colleges will even accept applicants on the spot! Summer is the best time to get on top of this process because for many colleges, once the time slots are filled, the opportunity is gone. Asking an art teacher for help is a good idea.

- Athletes should have their high school coach contact the college coaches on their behalf. They should provide their coach with a list of college coach names and contact information to streamline the process. Athletes should participate in any clinics or tournaments where college coaches are planning to attend. Many athletes will need to register with the clearinghouse at NCAA.org.

- Actors should get on the college's audition schedule as early as possible to ensure they have the opportunity to showcase their skills. Often colleges will offer local auditions as well. Actors do not want to miss this time and cost-saving opportunity.

Chapter 29

Stress-busters

"Why did they put this at the END of the book?"

- Reserve one night a week only to discuss the college process. This will preserve family dinner time and give everyone a much-needed break from thinking about the college process.

- The best way to beat stress is action. When your teenager is in a panic about the college process, redirect his or her nervous energy into an action step. Suggest that your teen visit a college website, begin that daunting first draft of the essay, or email admissions to set up an interview.

- Exercise is an effective way to alleviate the stress your teenager is harboring.

- Talk it out. Ask your teenager, "What is your biggest worry?" Then strategize ways to combat that concern.

- Enlist help from your teenager's college counselor. Emailing is a good method because your teenager can get all his or her concerns down in writing and let the counselor know exactly what is troubling him or her. Also, your teenager may feel more comfortable writing down his or her worries instead of voicing them in person.

- Choose a manageable course selection. The best strategy is to take the highest level classes that your teenager can handle, without "toppling the house of cards." You do not want to overload your teen to the point where all his or her classes suffer because he/she is spending an inordinate amount of time on that one AP class. Balance is key. Taking too many tough courses can cost your teen his or her emotional health which is not worth the price. Follow the guidance of your teen's current teachers to learn what level is most appropriate. If an AP course is not do-able, your teen might consider a consortium course (at a different high school), or a summer class at a community college. Any class that demonstrates intellectual curiosity is good.

- Consider hiring an independent college counselor. If your student's counselor is overloaded with students and your family cannot get the attention it needs, or if your student has a special situation, an independent counselor can be helpful.

Chapter 30

Worst Case Scenario

"Need we say more?"

- If your teenager is not accepted anywhere, what are his or her options? First of all, this rarely happens because you and your college counselor should ensure that your teenager has a balanced list which includes colleges where your teen is likely to be accepted. If this does happen, however, your counselor may have access to a listserv where colleges post openings. These openings occur when there is a discrepancy between the number of acceptances offered, and the number of students who enroll. Also, colleges experience "summer melt" where students decide to attend another college, thus creating an opening.

- If your teen is accepted, but a health issue or a family situation interferes with college attendance, your teen can usually defer for a year. This means that the college will hold a spot for your teen in the class which will be admitted the following year.

- If your teen is not ready to head off to college for any reason, there are a myriad of organized programs designed to provide teens with a meaningful, productive way to spend their time. Some of these programs involve community service, others are outdoor adventures, and still others involve travel. Ask your teen's college counselor for gap year programs. There are even consultants for finding the perfect program for your teen.

- If your financial situation changes unexpectedly, community college is another option for your teen. Many students attend community college for a year or two; credits can often transfer to four-year colleges.

Chapter 31

Financial Aid and Scholarships

"You expect me to PAY for this?"

- Net Price Calculator is a tool to help you calculate realistically the price of attending a specific institution (tuition, books, board, etc.). Many colleges have links to this tool on their websites, and the College Board website offers one as well.

- College is costly. The earlier your teenager understands this, the better. Make sure that your list includes some colleges which are more likely to offer your teen scholarships or merit aid. These would be colleges which are likely to accept your teen based on his/her test scores and GPA; use college counseling software like Naviance to see where students from your school have received scholarships in the past. Fastweb is another tool for investigating scholarships.

- Many colleges offer work-study programs as a way for students to make money while in school. Often these jobs are clerical in nature, with a good deal of down time where the student can study while on-the-job.

- Financial aid can be a test of your bargaining skills. Do

not be afraid to call College X and say that College Y has offered you more aid, and ask if they can match it. Once your teen is accepted, financial aid offices are more motivated to help get your teen enrolled.

- Be sure to let your college counselor know that you are very interested in scholarship opportunities. He or she will likely know which schools historically have offered students good financial aid packages and/or merit aid in the past.

Chapter 32

Early Action/Early Decision

"Do they have a Late or Really Late Plan?"

- Early action is when your student applies to one or more colleges near the start of senior year in hopes of getting an acceptance early in the process. November 1st is a popular deadline for many colleges. The advantage of early action is that a student can get a college acceptance in December instead of in March. Being accepted somewhere early in the process is an incredibly powerful stress-reliever. Early action is not binding; if a student is accepted to a college under the early action program, he or she may still apply to other colleges. Also, students may apply under the early action plan to several colleges at once. There is no disadvantage to applying early action, however, timing can be a challenge. Submitting an application by November 1st means that the entire application must be completed over the summer or in September, which is a very busy time for students academically. This option is ideal for highly-organized students who are self-motivated.

- Restrictive Early Action is similar to Early Action in that students hear an admit, defer or deny early in the year.

However, some colleges and universities have a policy where students may not apply to other colleges at the same time under Early Action or Early Decision. It is critical to read the fine print on applications about what is allowed.

- Early Decision is an early notification option which is binding. If a student is accepted under the Early Decision plan, the student must attend that college. Students sign a legal contract stating that it is their intention to attend the college if accepted. This is an option for students who are absolutely certain about their top choice college. Using Early Decision as a means to end the arduous college process early often results in unhappy students who end up transferring later. Admissions offices often provide statistical profiles of students admitted under the Early Decision plan from last year's cycle. Some colleges explain that it is harder to get admitted under Early Decision, while other colleges reveal that students who go this route often have a better chance of acceptance. It is worth researching how the college handles Early Decision applicants.

- Rolling deadlines are another terrific option. The basic premise here is that as soon as a student's application is received, the college will process it and make a decision, usually within four weeks of receiving the application. This often allows students to hear good news from colleges early in their school year as well.

- How many colleges should students apply to? Typically students apply to anywhere from 8 to 12 colleges. It is important to have a range of colleges on the list. For example, students should have at least one "reach" college where chances of admission are less likely, and at least two "likely" colleges where the student's profile is stronger than those of admitted students, thus suggesting that an acceptance would be "likely." The other colleges on the list should fall into the mid-range category where the students statistical profile (grades, scores, etc.) match the "mid-range" of accepted students. Students should use the admission statistics from college guidance books, admissions websites, and advice from their college counselors to determine how the colleges on their list should be categorized. Each application has a fee of about $75, so students should thoughtfully choose the colleges to be included on the list. If a student receives significant financial aid from his or her high school, he or she may qualify for application fee waivers. The college counselor has these waivers.

Appendix A

One-Week Study Schedule

Monday

8:00 am – Review for history test

8:30 am – Go to classes

3:00 pm – Break/change for practice

3:30 pm – Soccer practice

5:30 pm – Head home

6:00 pm – Eat dinner

7:00 pm – Begin homework – do HW assignments like math, grammar lesson, workbook page in Spanish, read history assignment actively and take notes

9:00 pm – Review for biology test

10:00 pm – Watch favorite show

10:30 pm – Go to bed

Tuesday

8:00 am (Before School) – Study notes for biology test

8:30 am – Go to classes

3:00 pm – Break/change for practice

3:30 pm – Soccer practice

5:30 pm – Head home

6:00 pm – Eat dinner

7:00 pm – Begin homework – do HW assignments like math, grammar lesson, workbook page in Spanish, read history assignment actively and take notes

9:00 pm – Begin outline of English paper due Monday

10:00 pm – Watch favorite show

10:30 pm – Go to bed

Wednesday

8:00 am – Meet with teacher about biology test on Tuesday

8:30 am – Go to classes

3:00 pm – Break/change for practice

3:30 pm – Soccer practice

5:30 pm – Head home

6:00 pm – Eat dinner

7:00 pm – Begin homework – do HW assignments like math, grammar lesson, workbook page in Spanish, read history assignment actively and take notes

9:00 pm – Review for biology test

10:00 pm – Watch favorite show

10:30 pm – Go to bed

Thursday

8:00 am – Meet with teacher about English paper due on Monday to make sure you are on the right track – show your teacher your opening paragraph

8:30 am – Go to classes

3:00 pm – Break/change for practice

3:30 pm – Soccer practice

5:30 pm – Head home

6:00 pm – Eat dinner

7:00 pm – Begin homework – do HW assignments like math, grammar lesson, workbook page in Spanish, read history assignment actively and take notes, write opening paragraph of essay

9:00 pm – Review for Spanish quiz and math quiz

10:00 pm – Watch favorite show

10:30 pm – Go to bed

Friday

8:00 am – Meet with history teacher about test on Tuesday. Check to make sure you have all the notes for the test and ask clarifying questions. Prepare the questions ahead of time.

8:30 am – Go to classes

3:00 pm – Break/change for practice

3:30 pm – Soccer practice

5:30 pm – Head home

6:00 pm – Eat dinner

7:00 pm – Go to the movies with friends

11:30 pm – Go to bed

Saturday

Write the rough draft of the English essay. Go over your notes for the history test.

Sunday

Do shorter assignments like math, science and language. Finalize your English paper. Study for the history test.

What to do if you get off schedule? It is kind of like going off a diet. You get right back on that horse. Be an advocate for yourself. If something comes up and you can't get the paper done or study for the test, talk to your teacher. See if it is possible to get an extension.

Appendix B

The College Organizational Tool

It is helpful to have an organizational tool to help you keep track of all of your colleges and their specific deadlines and requirements.

For each college you apply to, write down following information:

1. Is the SAT/ACT required or is this a test-optional school?
2. Have I sent scores? If so, record date.
3. What is the Early Decision deadline?
4. What is the Early Action Deadline?
5. What is the Regular Decision Deadline?
6. Is a supplement required?
7. What is the Application Fee?
8. Is an interview required?
9. Are SAT Subject Tests required?
10. Is the Common Application accepted?

Appendix C
Timeline for College Process

Freshman Year:

1. Focus on adjusting to the rigors of high school academics

2. Join extracurricular activities which interest you

3. Build friendships

4. Learn to self-advocate and see teachers for help

Sophomore Year:

1. Take the PSAT. This is typically offered at your school and does not require you to preregister on your own. Sometimes schools administer the test on Saturdays; be sure you will be in town. Making it up is tedious.

2. Do not prep for the PSAT. If your student is nervous, invest in a test prep book to get an idea of the types of questions, but save your money for prepping for the SAT/ACT. Colleges do not use these PSAT scores for admission. Think of the "P" in PSAT as practice.

3. Plan something productive for the summer: a job, an internship, community service, or summer course.

4. If family vacations take you near a college campus, plan a casual visit.

5. Start reading about colleges in *The Fiske Guide* and *The Insider's Guide to the Colleges*.

Junior Year:

1. Grades are critical this year. Academics are a priority.

2. Begin to formulate your list of colleges.

3. Plan a trip for spring break. Siblings benefit from coming along. If spring break is not an option for travel, plan long weekends for visits. Check your school policy about missing classes for college visits.

4. Visit your college counseling office for the school's internal timeline (when transcript requests need to be made, the process for teacher recommendations, etc.)

5. Think about which teachers you want to ask to write your recommendations. Ask them before the year ends as many will put a limit on how many they will write.

6. Take the ACT and SAT once each during the spring. Many students choose to take these tests in March since most schools have exams during the May/June testing dates.

7. Plan something productive for the summer.

8. Research prep classes/tutors/self-teach options for the summer.

9. Take SATIIs if your colleges require them.

Summer before Senior Year:

1. Prep for SAT/ACT using the score report to see which areas you need to focus on.

2. Write your college essay.

3. Start applications. Begin with a resume; follow with short answers and essay questions. Check to see if your colleges require a supplement. Complete those. Keep in mind that some supplements are brief while others may contain several short answers or more essays.

4. Fill out the College Organizational Tool (See Appendix B on page 107) with colleges and deadlines.

5. Finalize college lists. Be sure you have at least one likely school.

6. Fit in more visits if possible. Interview at colleges where recommended.

7. Register to retake SAT or ACT, if needed. Check which colleges require SATIIs and register for those.

8. Fill out the Common Application in its entirety. This will make all your applications—and the Common Application—go more smoothly.

9. Request transcripts from any other high schools or colleges from which you may have completed coursework (including summer school.) This takes time as you are not their priority—their own students are.

10. Parents: if your school allows you to submit a parent recommendation letter or a brag sheet, do so. This is your chance to contribute to your student's recommendation letter!

Senior Year:

1. Meet with your college counseling office early, before things get too busy, to make sure you are on track with the office's deadlines.

2. Retake ACT or SAT, if needed. Take any remaining required SAT IIs.

3. Give the teachers writing your recommendations a list of application deadlines, if needed.

4. Finalize applications as early as possible before the heavy academic workload builds.

5. If your school requires you to work with the registrar for transcripts, be sure to give the registrar a list of colleges to which you are applying.

6. Be sure to say hello to any college representatives visiting your school in the fall. If you cannot stay due to a lab or test, still say hello and fill out a contact card.

7. Prepare for your interviews by following our tips and researching the college's specific programs before you go.

8. Make a copy/print out all applications before submitting them—this is important whether you apply online or by mail.

About the Authors

Ginger Walsh Cobb has been an educator for over twenty-eight years. She attended the Brooks School in North Andover, Massachusetts. Ginger holds a B.A. in English from Denison University and an M.A. in Private School Leadership from Columbia University. Currently, Ginger is finishing her twenty-second year at St. Andrew's Episcopal School in Potomac, Maryland. She is the Head of Upper School, 10th Grade Academic Dean, and Co-Director of Service Learning. In her role as Head of Upper School, she educates students and their families on how to deal with drug and alcohol use, stress, harassment, abuse, Internet safety, eating disorders and depression. In her role as Academic Dean, she counsels students in selecting the right courses for their learning profile as well as helping them find a balance between academics, sports, activities, and friends. She teaches a service learning course where students engage in community service and learn more about themselves and the world. In her earlier years at St. Andrew's, Ginger was the Dean of Students, Athletic Director for Boys and Girls as well as the Director of Summer Programs. She taught high school and middle school English and coached Varsity Soccer and Lacrosse.

Ginger also has extensive experience in international education. She taught at the American School of Warsaw for

3 years and at the International Community School of Abidjan in Abidjan, Cote d'Ivoire for 2 years. Recently, Ginger traveled to Haiti with students and four other educators to begin a partnership with an impoverished school.

Ginger currently resides in Bethesda, MD with her husband and two children.

Kathleen Glynn-Sparrow launched and sustained a referral-only college counseling business for 5 years before co-creating The College Coaches, an eight year old business. Kathleen holds a B.A. from Duke University as well as a M.Ed. from Emory University. She has been in education for 18 years. Kathleen was Director of College Counseling and 11th Grade Academic Dean at St. Andrew's Episcopal School in Potomac, MD. She continues to teach the highly in-demand course "The College Essay and Application." Her experience as a high school English teacher enables her to help students transform their essays from a wisp of an idea to a finished piece.

Kathleen has counseled students from Gonzaga, Stone Ridge, NCS, Whitman, Churchill, The Academy of the Holy Cross, Maret, Wootton, Sandy Spring, St. Andrew's, St. Jane, St. John's and Good Counsel. She has been a returning guest speaker at Churchill High School on "How to Market Your Internship to Colleges." She has traveled extensively allowing her to advise students on colleges that she has personally visited. Kathleen furthered her knowledge of college counseling at the Harvard Admissions Institute.

Prior to St. Andrew's, Kathleen taught at The Ben Franklin Academy in Atlanta, GA. There she counseled students challenged with learning disabilities, substance abuse recovery and motivational issues.

Currently, Kathleen is the Associate Director of College Counseling at Stone Ridge School of the Sacred Heart in Bethesda, MD, where she also served as Chair of the English Department. Kathleen lives in suburban Maryland with her husband and two children.

45947454R00068

Made in the USA
Middletown, DE
18 July 2017